Contents

There are many types of animals.

Creature Comparisons

ds

Tracey Crawford

Heinemann
LIBRARY

www.heinemann.co.uk/library
Visit our website to find out more information about Heinemann Library books.

To order:
- ☎ Phone 44 (0) 1865 888066
- Send a fax to 44 (0) 1865 314091
- 📄 Visit the Heinemann Bookshop at www.heinemann.co.uk/library to browse our
- 💻 catalogue and order online.

First published in Great Britain by Heinemann Library,
Halley Court, Jordan Hill, Oxford OX2 8EJ, part of Harcourt
Education. Heinemann is a registered trademark of Harcourt
Education Ltd.

© Harcourt Education Ltd 2007
First published in paperback in 2007
The moral right of the proprietor has been asserted.

Editorial: Tracey Crawford, Cassie Mayer, Dan Nunn,
and Sarah Chappelow
Design: Jo Hinton-Malivoire
Picture Research: Tracy Cummins and Tracey Engel,
and Ruth Blair
Production: Duncan Gilbert

Originated by Chroma Graphics (Overseas) Pte. Ltd
Printed and bound in China by South China
Printing Company

ISBN 978 0 431 18225 4 (hardback)
11 10 09 08 07
10 9 8 7 6 5 4 3 2 1

ISBN 978 0 431 18348 0 (paperback)
12 11 10 09 08
10 9 8 7 6 5 4 3 2 1

British Library Cataloguing in Publication Data
Crawford, Tracey
  Birds. - (Creature comparisons)
  1.Birds - Juvenile literature
  I.Title
  598

Acknowledgements
The publishers would like to thank the following for permission to
reproduce photographs: Corbis pp. 4 (monkey, Frank Lukasseck),
5 (Arthur Morris), 6 (W. Perry Conway), 8 (pelican, Theo Allofs),
10 (Farrell Grehan), 11 (Paul A. Souders), 16 (Joe McDonald), 18
(Tom Brakefield), 19 (Arthur Morris), 22 (penguins, Tim Davis; egret,
Royalty Free), 23 (seagull eggs, Farrell Grehan; baby birds, Paul A.
Souders); Getty Images pp. 4 (fish), 8 (macaw, Digital Vision; eagle,
PhotoDisc), 12 (JH Pete Carmichael), 13 (Johnny Johnson), 14 (Don
Klumpp), 15 (Roy Toft); NHPA p. 17 (Andy Rouse); Carlton Ward pp.
4 (snake, frog), 7, 8 (tropical bird), 20, 21.

Cover photograph of an emperor penguin reproduced with permission of photolibrary.com/Mark Jones and a blue parrot reproduced
with permission of Corbis/Royalty Free. Back cover photograph of a
laughing gull reproduced with permission of Getty Images/JH Pete
Carmichael.

Every effort has been made to contact copyright holders of any
material reproduced in this book. Any omissions will be rectified in
subsequent printings if notice is given to the publishers.

Birds are one type of animal.

All birds have feathers.

All birds have two wings.

All birds have a beak.

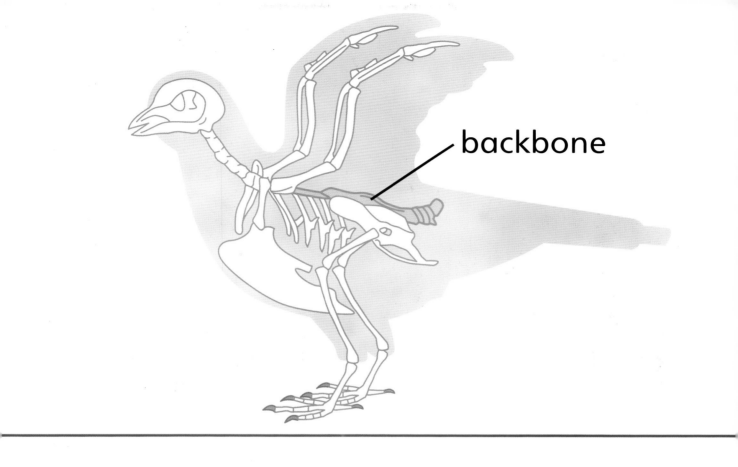

backbone

All birds have a backbone.

egg

All baby birds hatch from an egg.

nest

All baby birds live in a nest.

Most birds can fly.

But these birds cannot fly.

Some birds are big.

Some birds are small.

Some birds fly high.

Some birds fly low.

Some birds swim.

Some birds dive.

Every bird is different.

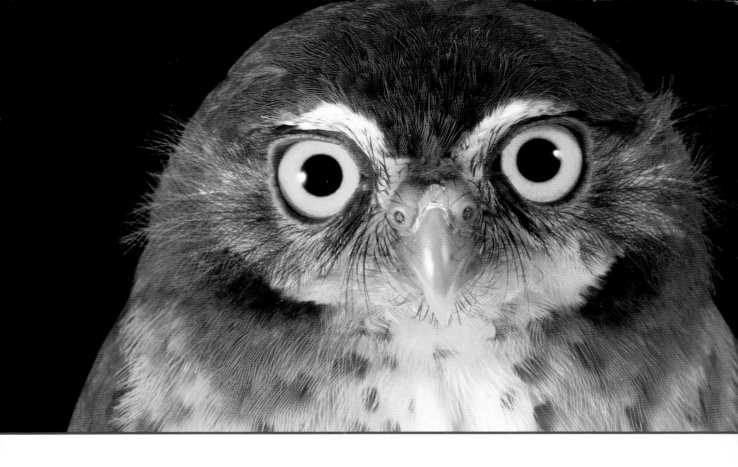

Every bird is special.

Bird facts

Birds that can fly have very light bones. This helps them fly.

Penguins use their wings like paddles. This helps them swim.

Picture glossary

backbone the part of the skeleton that goes from the head to the tail

hatch to be born from an egg

nest the home where a baby bird is born

Index

Notes to parents and teachers
Before reading
Talk to the children about birds. Does anyone keep a pet bird? What different birds can they name?

After reading
Sing the nursery rhyme: "Two little dicky birds sitting on a wall. One named Peter, the other named Paul. Fly away Peter. Fly away Paul. Come back Peter. Come back Paul." Show children the hand actions to go with the rhyme, using a thumb for each of the birds which fly behind the children's backs.
Make a pine cone bird feeder: Tie a long piece of thin string to the top of the cone. Mix together some lard and plenty of porridge oats. Add some sunflower seeds and chopped dried fruit. Roll the pine cone in the mixture. Hang the bird feeder outside.
Make a CD bird: Make tail feathers from strips of brightly coloured paper and tape them to an unwanted CD. Make two wings from coloured paper and tape these on either side of the CD. Use a "V"-shaped piece of yellow card for the beak. Cut a small opening in the back of the beak and fix on the edge of the CD. Put two dots for eyes on the CD. Suspend the "birds" from the ceiling.